ANGULAR

INTERVIEW QUESTIONS AND ANSWERS

Copyrights

Angular Interview Question and Answers

Copyright © 2021 by Vishal garg. All rights reserved

vishgeek@gmail.com

About the Book

Angular interview questions is designed to help readers learn the basic concepts of Angular.

This book covers all the concepts of Angular with the help of Interview question and Answers.

Most Questions are included in this book which are frequently asked in current scenario.

Contents

Q1. What is Angular ?

- Angular is a JavaScript framework written in typescript.
- Single page applications (SPA) are build using Angular
- Web, desktop and mobile applications are build by using Angular

Q2. Why Angular?

1. Automatic Synchronization :-

Angular provides **Two-way binding** using which data is automatically synchronized between model(typescript component) and view (html template).

2. Reusability :-

The **component** based architecture of Angular makes the code reusable across whole application.

3.Ease of unit testing :-

Since we have **independent components**, unit testing is much easier in angular applications.

4.Modular Structure :-

Modules make angular application easy to maintain and also provides benefits of lazy loading i.e. to load the features on-demand

5.Typescript :-

Angular application is built in Typescript (a superset of JavaScript). Typescript provides more features in terms of type checking, early error catching, debugging etc.

6.Efficient :-

Angular provides highly optimized bundle sizes. It has smaller file sizes and hence faster component loading.

7.Ease of Maintenance :-

Decoupled components are easy to maintain i.e. they can be easily replaced, removed or added. This makes updates in application easy.

Q3. What are Angular CLI Schematics ?

To add or update something in project

1. **ng generate** :- Generate components, services, routes using CLI commands
2. **ng add** :- Add third party libraries in a project
3. **ng update** :- update package or libraries in project

Angular builders

1. **ng build** :- compile the application
2. **ng lint** :- check quality of code
3. **ng deploy** :- deploy the application

Q4. Name some frequently used CLI commands and their purpose ?

Commands	Purpose
Ng new <Project name>	Create New Project
Ng serve	Test the application
Ng serve --o	Build and run the application
Ng build	Compile the application
Ng build --prod	Create Dist folder to deploy code to production environment
Ng deploy <Project name>	Deploy the application
Ng **g c** <Component name>	Generate the Component in application with .spec and .css files
Ng **g c** --skipTests=true --s <Component name>	Generate Component without .spec and .css files
Ng **g s** <Service name>	Generate Service
Ng **g s** --skiptests=true <Service name>	Generate Service without .spec file
Ng **g cl** <Model name> --type=model	Generate Model class

Ng add <Library name>	Add 3rd part libraries e.g.:- @angular/material
Ng update	To update project packages and libraries
Ng lint	Check quality of code

Q5. What is a purpose of package.json file ?

package.json is a json file which holds the metadata information and manages projects' dependencies , version, script etc.

Dependencies packages in package.json are :-

- **Angular packages** - Angular core packages(@angular/)
- **3rd party packages** - 3rd party libraries required in application
- **polyfill packages** - polyfills emulates features which are missing in some browsers.

Q6. What is a purpose of tsconfig.json file?

It contains instructions to convert or transpile typescript file(.ts) to JavaScript file(.js). The tsconfig.json file contains the root files and the compiler options required to compile the project.

Furthermore, there are some more variants of tsconfig.json : -

- **tsconfig.base.json** :- Contains information on the compiler
- **tsconfig.app.json** :- Contains configuration information for the application
- **tsconfig.spec.json** :- Contains typescript configuration for the **Tests** in application. Like, **Jasmine** is used for testing.

Q7. What is a purpose of tslint.json file?

Tslint.json file contains the linting configuration for the application. Linting is a tool to flag errors, style errors, best practices errors, bugs etc.

Q8. What is a purpose of angular.json file ?

Contains project specific configuration. It defines structure of application and includes project settings.

Some of the settings are :-

- **Environment** :- Environment settings like (development, production) is specified here
- **Styles and Scripts :-** Styles and scripts settings are also added here. Bootstrap files are also added here
- **Root files** :- Root files settings are also included here
- **Compiler :-** Complier settings are also included here. Like we can set AOT complier true or false from here
- **Resources :-** Resource settings like any icons, images or assets are also included here
- **Test :-** Test settings are included here
- **Lint :-** Lint settings are included here
- **Project information** :- It contains version, schematic etc. information

Q9. What is Karma.config.js ?

It contains the **testing tools** required for the project, the environment for testing and any specific action which may be required for testing purpose.

Q10. What is a purpose of node_modules ?

This folder contains the **libraries downloaded from npm.** This folder should not be deployed as it automatically download packages from package.json.

Q11. Why we have a "src" folder in a project ?

This folder contains the main code files like components (.ts), modules, templates(.html), stylesheets(.css), environment configuration etc.

Q12. Which file bootstraps whole application ?

Main.ts

- The code in the main.ts file gets executed first
- Main.ts creates a browser environment for application
- This file bootstraps(starts) the whole application by passing App module from app.module.ts

Q13. What is a entry file in Angular application ?

index.html

index.html is a entry file which contains the root level component of whole application.

It contains a root level component.

e.g. <app-root></app-root>

Q14. Polyfill.ts . Explain?

This file contains code that is used to provide **compatibility support for older browsers**. polyfills fills the missing features of browsers that do not support latest versions of JavaScript specifications.

Q15. Where we store Global CSS for whole App ?

Styles.css is a **Global CSS** file for whole Angular application.

Q16. Where we store resources of a Project ?

Assets folder contains the resource files like images, icons, locales etc. which are used in application.

Q17. Why do we need "App" folder in a Application ?

This folder contains the components, modules files which you have created for your Angular application.

Q18. Routing configuration can be stored in which module file ?

app-routing.module.ts

This module file contains **routing configuration** and it is loaded from root module i.e. app.module.ts. Though routing configuration can be placed in root module (app.module.ts) as well but it is best practice to place routing configuration in separate module file.

Q19. Which files are associated with a Component ?

app.component.css :-

This file contains **CSS styles** for app component

app.component.html :-

This file contains the **view** of component. It is a template which is used corresponding to a component (typescript file).

app.component.spec.ts :-

This file is a **unit testing** file corresponding to a app component. It is executed by Angular CLI command (ng test).

app.component.ts :-

This is a **component** file written in typescript which contains the logic of component.

Q20. What is Main module of a Application ?

app.module.ts

This is a **main module** file written in typescript which includes all the
dependencies of a application. All the modules, components, root component are
registered here.

Q21. Explain the Flow of Angular Application ?

1. **Angular.json:** Angular.json Contains all configurations of Angular
   application. Builder look into this file for all the paths and configurations to
   load main file(main.ts)
2. **Main.ts:** Main.ts is a entry point of a application. It calls the function
   bootstrapModule(AppModule)
3. **App.module.ts:** This a main module file which bootstraps the main
   component file like AppComponent
4. **App.component.ts:** In app.module.ts we are bootstrapping
   Appcomponent(App.component.ts). This is a main component file which
   contains the logic (.ts file) and template(.html file)
5. **Index.html:** Angular app is aware of all the modules, components, styles,
   scripts of the application at this point. Now, index.html is executed which
   contains root component app-root
6. **App.component.html:** This file contains all the html elements. Contents of
   this file are displayed at the start of a application.

Q22. What are the key components of Angular ?

Key components of an Angular Application are : -

1. Components
2. Modules
3. Data Binding
4. Directives
5. Templates
6. Metadata
7. Services and Dependency Injection

Q23. What are Components ?

Components are basic building blocks in a angular application

- Components are normal **typescript class**
- Defined by **@Component decorator**
- Consists of Class and Metadata
- Metadata consists of selector, template, style and other properties
- Template is a UI design of page (.html file)
- Selector is a unique name by which component is identified in Html DOM

e.g :

```
import { Component } from '@angular/core';

@Component({
  selector: 'app-root',
  templateUrl: './app.component.html',
  styleUrls: ['./app.component.css']
})
export class AppComponent {
  title = 'NewApp';
}
```

Q24. What are Modules ?

- Module is a **bundling of building blocks** like components, directives, pipes, routes, services.
- **@NgModule decorator** is used to create a module class
- One **root module** is always required in angular application
- Module can be split into **multiple modules** like we can have routing module which handles routing feature only and this module is then included in root module
- Every component of a application needs to be registered in a module

Q25. Can you explan ngModule Decorator ?

@NgModule decorator is used to create a module class

NgModule has 4 properties:-

1. **declarations** : register every component here
2. **imports** : import every module here
3. **providers**: provide services used in app
4. **bootstrap**: root component of app

e.g.
```
import { MaterialModule } from './material/material.module';
import { BrowserModule } from '@angular/platform-browser';
import { NgModule } from '@angular/core';

import { AppRoutingModule } from './app-routing.module';
import { AppComponent } from './app.component';
import { BrowserAnimationsModule } from '@angular/platform-browser/animations';

@NgModule({
  declarations: [AppComponent],
  imports: [
    BrowserModule,
    AppRoutingModule,
    BrowserAnimationsModule,
    MaterialModule
  ],
  providers: [],
  bootstrap: [AppComponent],
})
export class AppModule {}
```

Q26. Can you create a separate module apart from root module ?

Yes, we can create multiple modules apart from root module.

Every module is a standalone module i.e. you need to export the module to root module in order to use that module at application level.

e.g. :- We can create separate routing module , but we still need to export this routing module to our root module(app module)

[app-routing.module.ts]

import { NgModule } from '@angular/core';

import { Routes, RouterModule } from '@angular/router';

const routes: Routes = [];

@NgModule({

  imports: [RouterModule.forRoot(routes)],

  exports: [RouterModule]

})

export class AppRoutingModule { }

Q27. What are Data Bindings ?

Data binding is a process of establishing a connection between user interface template (Html file) and its component(typescript file)

Using Data binding typescript code (business logic) communicates with its template (user interface)

Data binding = Communication

Q28. What are types of Data Bindings ?

1. String Interpolation (One-way Binding)
2. Property Binding (One-way Binding)
3. Event Binding (One-way Binding)
4. Two-Way Binding

Q29. What is a ONE-WAY Binding ?

ONE-WAY :- Data is passed from one side only.

It can further be categorized as : -

1. **Output** :- Data is passed from **typescript to html**
   Example of Output one-way binding are : -
   - **String Interpolation**
   - **Property Binding**

2. **Input** :- Data is passed from **html to typescript**
   Example of Input one-way binding is : -
   - **Event Binding**

Q30. What is a TWO-WAY Binding ?

Two-Way :- Data is communicated from both sides i.e. template(.html) and component(.ts). It is a **Combination** of both **(event)** and **[property]** bindings.

Q31. What is String Interpolation ?

- String Interpolation is a type of **one-way data binding** which is used to pass data from **typescript to template** (html).
- Changes made in typescript updates the property in html
- Everything inside curly braces {{}} is interpreted as a string

Syntax :- {{propertyName}}

Q32. What is Property Binding ?

- Property Binding is a type of **one-way data binding** which is used to dynamically bind DOM properties of html elements.
- Changes made in typescript updates the property in html

Syntax :- [propertyName]

e.g.
[app.component.html]
```html
<div>
 <p><input type="text" [value]= title [disabled]=isTrue></p>
</div>
```

[app.component.ts]
```typescript
import { Component } from '@angular/core';

@Component({
 selector: 'app-root',
 templateUrl: './app.component.html',
 styleUrls: ['./app.component.css']
})
export class AppComponent {
 title = 'Property binding';
 isTrue = true;
}
```

Q33. What is Event Binding ?

- Event Binding capture events raised in template (html file) and a event handler in component (typescript class) will handle these events
- Data from events is passed from **template to typescript**
- **$event** can be passed as argument in (event) to access event data

Syntax :- (eventName)

[app.component.html]
```html
<div>
 <p><input type="text" [value]= title [disabled]=isTrue></p>
</div>
<div>
 <button (click)="onChange()">Change title</button>
</div>
```

[app.component.ts]
```typescript
import { Component } from '@angular/core';
@Component({
```

```
  selector: 'app-root',
  templateUrl: './app.component.html',
  styleUrls: ['./app.component.css'],
})
export class AppComponent {
 title = 'one way binding';
 isTrue = true;
 onChange(): void {
   this.title = 'event binding';
 }
}
```

Q34. How TWO-WAY Binding is implemented?

- In Two way data binding data is communicated from component(typescript) to view(html) and vice- versa.
- It's a combination of both (event) and [property] binding
  (event) + [property] = [(Two way binding)]
- **ngModel** directive is used for two-way data binding
- **FormsModule** library needs to be imported in App.module.ts as ngModel is not a part of angular library

Syntax :- [(ngModel)]

```
e.g.
[app.module.ts]
import { BrowserModule } from '@angular/platform-browser';
import { NgModule } from '@angular/core';

import { AppRoutingModule } from './app-routing.module';
import { AppComponent } from './app.component';
import { FormsModule } from '@angular/forms';

@NgModule({
  declarations: [AppComponent],
  imports: [BrowserModule, AppRoutingModule, FormsModule],
  providers: [],
  bootstrap: [AppComponent],
```

```
})
export class AppModule {}
```

[app.component.html]
```html
<div>
  <p><input type="text" [value]= title [(ngModel)]="title"></p>
</div>
<p>
  <label>New title is : </label>
  <input type="text" [value]= title>
</p>
```

[app.component.ts]
```typescript
import { Component } from '@angular/core';

@Component({
  selector: 'app-root',
  templateUrl: './app.component.html',
  styleUrls: ['./app.component.css'],
})
export class AppComponent {
  title = 'two way binding';
}
```

Q35. How to pass data between Components ?

A parent component cannot access the properties of child component because in angular the scope of property is limited to its component only. Even parent component cannot access the properties of child component

To share data between parent and child components, we can use 2 properties provided by angular -

- **@input()**
- **@output()**

Q36. What is @input() Property?

- @Input() property is used to pass data from **Parent component to child component**
- Use **@Input() decorator** with a property in **child component** in order to receive data from parent component
- Import **Input** from **'@angular/core'** library
- **Syntax:- @Input() propertyName;**

e.g.
[**child.component.ts**]
```
import { Component, Input } from '@angular/core';

@Component({
  selector: 'app-child',
  templateUrl: './child.component.html',
  styles: [],
})
export class ChildComponent {
  constructor() {}
  @Input() childProperty = 'default child component';
}
```

[**child.component.html**]
```
<div style="border: 1px solid;"><h4>child component</h4>
<input type="text" [value]= childProperty>
</div>
```

[**app.component.ts – Parent Component**]
```
import { Component } from '@angular/core';

@Component({
  selector: 'app-root',
```

```
  templateUrl: './app.component.html',
  styleUrls: ['./app.component.css'],
})
export class AppComponent {
  title = 'Input property';
}
```

[app.component.html]

```html
<div style="border: 1px solid">
  <h4>parent component</h4>
  <p><input type="text" [value]="title" [(ngModel)]="title" /></p>

  <p>
    <app-child [childProperty]="title"></app-child>
  </p>
</div>
```

Note* :

<app-child> - is a child component directive .

[childProperty] - It's a property of child component which is accessible here because of @Input() decorator in child component.

Q37. Can you use Alias name in @input() property ?

We can assign alias name to the property using @input()

Syntax:- @Input('aliasName') propertyName;

Q38. What is @Output() Property ?

- @Output() property is used to pass data from **child component to parent component**

- Create a custom event in child component to emit values to its parent component
- **EventEmitter** is used to create a custom events
- Use **@Output() decorator** with a event property in **child component** in order to emit data to parent component
- Import **output** from '**@angular/core**' library
- Import **EventEmitter** from '**@angular/core**' library
- **Syntax:- @Output() eventName = new EventEmitter<T>();**

e.g.

[child.component.ts - Child Component]

```typescript
import { Component, EventEmitter, Output } from '@angular/core';

@Component({
  selector: 'app-child-output',
  templateUrl: './child-output.component.html',
  styleUrls: ['./child-output.component.css'],
})
export class ChildOutputComponent {
  constructor() {}
  textValue = 'default';
  @Output() childProperty = new EventEmitter<string>();

  AddToParent(item: string): void {
    this.childProperty.emit(item);
  }
}
```

[child.component.html]

```html
<div style="border: 1px solid">
  <h4>child component</h4>
  <input type="text" [value]="textValue" [(ngModel)]="textValue" />
</div>
```

```html
<div>
  <button (click)="AddToParent(textValue)">Add to Parent</button>
</div>
```

[app.component.html – Parent component]

```html
<div style="border: 1px solid">
  <h4>parent component</h4>
  <p><input type="text" [value]="title" [(ngModel)]="title" /></p>

  <p>
    <app-child (childProperty)="GetValue($event)"></app-child>
  </p>
</div>
```

[app.component.ts – Parent component]

```typescript
import { Component } from '@angular/core';

@Component({
  selector: 'app-root',
  templateUrl: './app.component.html',
  styleUrls: ['./app.component.css'],
})
export class AppComponent {
  title = 'Input property';
  GetValue(event: string) {
    this.title = event;
  }
}
```

Q39. How to Alias a @Output() property ?

We can assign alias name to the property using @Output()

Syntax:- @Output('aliasName') propertyName;

Q40. How can we pass styles from parent to child component ?

ViewEncapsulation

- Styles applied to particular component are not overridden to child components
- Add **Encapsulation** property in @Component directive to override styles to child components
- Import **ViewEncapsulation** from '@angular/core' library

e.g.

@Component({

 selector: 'app-root',

 templateUrl: './app.component.html',

 styleUrls: ['./app.component.css'],

 encapsulation: ViewEncapsulation.None

})

ViewEncapsulation.None :- It will apply all parent component styles to child

VIewEncapsulation.Emulated(Default) :- Parent component styles will not override styles of child component.

Q41. What is Local reference in a template ?

- Local reference variable will hold the reference of whole html element and all its properties
- Scope of local reference variable is limited to its template only

Syntax:- #variableName

[app.component.html]

<div id="pd" style="border: 1px solid">

 <h4>parent component</h4>

```html
<p><input type="text" [value]="title" #name /></p>

<p>

  <app-child-output (childProperty)="GetValue(name)"></app-child-output>

</p>

<p>Local ref. value is : {{ title }}</p>

</div>
```

[app.component.ts]
```typescript
import { Component } from '@angular/core';

@Component({
 selector: 'app-root',
 templateUrl: './app.component.html',
 styleUrls: ['./app.component.css']
 })
export class AppComponent {
 title = 'Input property';

 GetValue(element: HTMLInputElement) {
  this.title = element.value;
 }
}
```

Q42. What is ViewChild?

- Html DOM elements can be accessed in typescript file by using ViewChild decorator
- Local reference variable or component name can be passed as argument in ViewChild
- **Import ViewChild** from '@angular/core'
- **Syntax: @ViewChild(reference selector, { static: true }) variableName: ElementRef;**

e.g.
[app.component.ts]
```typescript
import { Component, ElementRef, ViewChild } from '@angular/core';

@Component({
 selector: 'app-root',
 templateUrl: './app.component.html',
 styleUrls: ['./app.component.css'],
})
export class AppComponent {
 title = 'Input property';
 @ViewChild('name', { static: true }) name: ElementRef;

 GetValue() {
   this.title = this.name.nativeElement.value;
 }
}
```

```html
[app.component.html]
<div id="pd" style="border: 1px solid">
<h4>parent component</h4>
<p><input type="text" [value]="title" #name /></p>
<p>
<app-child-output (childProperty)="GetValue()"></app-child-output>
</p>
<p>Local ref. value is : {{title}}</p>
</div>
```

Q43. What is ng-content ?

- ng-content is used to place content inside component's opening and closing tag
- By default, any content inside component will be lost
- ng-content acts as placeholder to project content into components

Syntax: <ng-content>

[app.component.html – Parent component]

```
<div id="pd" style="border: 1px solid">
 <h4>parent component</h4>
 <p>
  <app-child(childProperty)="GetValue()">Test data here</app-child>
 </p>
</div>
```

Note* : This data "**Test data here**" will be lost. <ng-content> should be used to project this content inside component

[child.component.html - child component]

```
<div style="border: 1px solid">
 <h4>child component</h4>
 <ng-content></ng-content>
</div>
```

Note* : **<ng-content>** is a Placeholder. 'Test data here' will be projected here.

Q44. What is ContentChild ?

- Element or component inside <ng-content> can be accessed in typescript file by using ContentChild decorator
- Local reference variable or component name can be passed as argument in ContentChild
- Import **ContentChild** from '@angular/core'
- **Syntax: @ContentChild(reference selector, { static: true }) variableName: ElementRef;**

e.g.

[app.component.html - parent component]

```
<div id="pd" style="border: 1px solid">
 <h4>parent component</h4>
 <p>
  <app-child (childProperty)="GetValue()">
   <p #varName>
   Test data here
```

```html
    </p>
  </app-child>
 </p>
</div>
```

[child.component.html - child component]

```html
<div style="border: 1px solid">
 <h4>child component</h4>
 <ng-content></ng-content>
</div>


<div>
 <button (click)="AddToParent(textValue)">Add to Parent</button>
</div>
```

[child.component.ts - child component]

```typescript
import {
 Component,
 ContentChild,
 ElementRef,
 EventEmitter,
 Output,
} from '@angular/core';

@Component({
 selector: 'app-child',
 templateUrl: './child-output.component.html',
 styleUrls: ['./child-output.component.css'],
})
export class ChildOutputComponent {
 constructor() {}
 textValue = 'default';

 @Output() childProperty = new EventEmitter<string>();
 @ContentChild('varName', { static: true }) varName: ElementRef;

 AddToParent(item: string): void {
```

```
    this.childProperty.emit(item);

    console.log('content child value: ' +
    this.varName.nativeElement.textContent);
    }
}
```

Q45. What are Lifecycle Hooks ?

- Lifecycle hooks are events which gets triggered at specific points of component's life
- There are 8 stages in a life cycle of a component
- These 8 life cycle hooks gets triggered in a sequential order

Q46. Can you tell in which order Lifecycle hooks are triggered ?

8 life cycle hooks in sequential order in which they are triggered are :-

1. **ngOnChanges**
2. **ngOnInit**
3. **ngDoCheck**
4. **ngAfterContentInit**
5. **ngAfterContentChecked**
6. **ngAfterViewInit**
7. **ngAfterViewChecked**
8. **ngOnDestroy**

Q47. Tell me about ngOnChanges ?

<u>ngOnChanges</u>

- Called every time a data-bound **Input Property** changes
- It is the **first hook** to be called in a lifecycle
- It's the only hook which receives an argument.

- It receives a **SimpleChanges** object which contains previous and current values of a input property
- **OnChanges** interface should be implemented
- import **OnChanges** and **SimpleChanges** from **'@angular/core'** library

e.g.

[child.component.ts]

```typescript
import { OnChanges, SimpleChanges } from '@angular/core';
import { Component, Input, OnInit } from '@angular/core';

@Component({
  selector: 'app-child',
  templateUrl: './child.component.html',
  styles: [],
})
export class ChildComponent implements OnInit, OnChanges {
  @Input() childElement: string;
  constructor() {
    console.log('constructor called');
  }
  ngOnChanges(changes: SimpleChanges): void {
    console.log('ngOnChanges called : ' + changes);
  }
  ngOnInit(): void {
    console.log('ngOnInit called');
  }
}
```

[child.component.html]

```html
<div>
  <p>Child Component</p>
  <p><input type="text" [value]="childElement"></p>
</div>
```

[app.component.ts]

```typescript
import { Component } from '@angular/core';
```

```
@Component({
  selector: 'app-root',
  templateUrl: './app.component.html',
  styleUrls: ['./app.component.css'],
})
export class AppComponent {
 title = 'LifeCycle';

 Change(name: string): void {
   this.title = name;
  }
}
```

[app.component.html]
```
<div>
 <p>Parent Component</p>
 <input type="text" [value]="title" #name>
 <p><button (click)="Change(name.value)">Change</button></p>
 <p><app-child [childElement]="title"></app-child></p>
</div>
```

Q48. Tell me about ngOnInit ?

- Called on initialization of a component
- It is the called **after** the **Constructor**.
- **OnInit** interface should be implemented
- import **OnInit** from **'@angular/core'** library

Q49. Tell me about ngOnCheck ?

- Called at every change detection cycle
- Use this hook instead of **ngOnChanges** as it may conflict if both hooks are used together
- **DoCheck** interface should be implemented
- import **DoCheck** from **'@angular/core'** library

Q50. What is ngAfterContentInit Hook ?

- Called after content(ng-content) is projected in the component
- **AfterContentInit** interface should be implemented
- import **AfterContentInit** from **'@angular/core'** library

Q51. What is ngAfterContentChecked Hook ?

- Called after projected content(ng-content) is checked
- **AfterContentChecked** interface should be implemented
- import **AfterContentChecked** from **'@angular/core'** library

Q52. What is ngAfterViewInit Hook ?

- Called after a component's view(or child view) is initialized
- **AfterViewInit** interface should be implemented
- import **AfterViewInit** from **'@angular/core'** library

Q53. Tell me about ngAfterViewChecked Hook ?

- Called after a component's view(or child view) is checked
- **AfterViewChecked** interface should be implemented
- import **AfterViewChecked** from **'@angular/core'** library

Q54. Tell me about ngOnDestroy Hook ?

- Called once a component is about to get destroyed
- Mainly used for cleanup and unsubscribe purposes
- **OnDestroy** interface should be implemented
- import **OnDestroy** from **'@angular/core'** library

Q55. What are Directives and their Types ?

Directives are instructions which gets executed whenever compiler finds it in DOM

There are 3 types of directives

1. **Component Directive** -
   - Directives with templates.
   - These directives have their own custom HTML attached with them

2. **Structural Directive** -
   - DOM layout is changed i.e. an element is added or not to a DOM structure
   - Structural directives are prefixed with asterisk(*) symbol.
   - e.g. ***ngIf** and ***ngfor** are structural directives

3. **Attribute Directive** -
   - Appearance or behavior of an element, component etc. is changed
   - e.g. **ngStyle**

Q56. Tell me about Component Directive ?

These are custom directives i.e. in this directive a custom template is attached corresponding to a component.

e.g.
[directive.component.ts]

```
import { Component, OnInit } from '@angular/core';

@Component({
  selector: 'app-directive',
  templateUrl: './directive.component.html',
  styles: [],
})
export class DirectiveComponent implements OnInit {
  constructor() {}

  ngOnInit(): void {}
}
```

[directive.component.html]
```
<p>directive works!</p>
```

[app.component.html]
```
<p>Hello App component !!</p>
<app-directive></app-directive>
```

Note* : <app-directive></app-directive> acts as a placeholder. business logic and template from component (directive.component.ts) is replaced here.

Q57. What is Structural Directive ?

These are pre-defined directives which manipulates the html DOM.
Structural Directive changes the DOM structure i.e. it adds or removes html elements from DOM structure.
Some commonly used Structural directives are -

- ***ngIf**
- ***ngFor**
- **ngSwitch**

***ngIf -**

- It's a conditional statement i.e. show or hide some html elements based on a condition.

e.g.
[.Html file]
```
<div *ngIf="items.length > 0">
Success - There are items in List
</div>
<div *ngIf="items.length === 0">
Failure - There are no items in List
</div>
```

[.ts file]
```
import { Component, OnInit } from '@angular/core';
```

```typescript
@Component({
  selector: 'app-directive',
  templateUrl: './directive.component.html',
  styles: [],
})
export class DirectiveComponent implements OnInit {
constructor() {}
items = [];

ngOnInit(): void {}
}
```

*ngIf with else -

We can also add else with *ngIf to show or hide html elements based on conditions. But to use else condition we need ng-template directive

Q58. What is ng-template ?

It acts as a placeholder for if else conditions.

[.html file]

```html
<div *ngIf="items.length > 0 ; then success else failure">

</div>
<ng-template #success>

  Success - There are items in List

</ng-template>
<ng-template #failure>

  Failure - There are no items in List

</ng-template>
```

[.ts file]
```typescript
import { Component, OnInit } from '@angular/core';

@Component({
  selector: 'app-directive',
  templateUrl:
  './directive.component.html',
  styles: [],
})
export class DirectiveComponent
implements OnInit {
  constructor() {}
  items = [1, 2];

  ngOnInit(): void {}
}
```

Q59. What is *ngFor directive ?

*ngFor directive is used for iterating list of objects.

e.g.

[.html file]
```html
<div *ngIf="items.length > 0 ; then success else failure">
</div>
<ng-template #success>
  Success - There are items in List
<ul>
<li *ngFor="let item of items">{{item}}
</li>
</ul>
</ng-template>
<ng-template #failure>
  Failure - There are no items in List
</ng-template>
```

[.ts file]
```typescript
import { Component, OnInit } from '@angular/core';
```

```typescript
@Component({
  selector: 'app-directive',
  templateUrl:
   './directive.component.html',
  styles: [],
})
export class DirectiveComponent
implements OnInit {
  constructor() {}
  items = [1, 2];


  ngOnInit(): void {}
}
```

Q60. Tell me about ngSwitch directive ?

- Show or hide one element from list of elements based on a condition.
- ngSwitch uses property binding instead of asterisk(*)
- ngSwitch is a structural directive consists of 2 more structural directives - *ngSwitchCase and *ngSwitchDefault

[.html file]

```html
<div [ngSwitch]="color">

<div *ngSwitchCase="'RED'">Color is Red</div>

<div *ngSwitchCase="'BLUE'">Color is Blue</div>

<div *ngSwitchDefault>Default Color is Black</div>

</div>
```

[.ts file]

```typescript
import { Component, OnInit } from '@angular/core';
```

```
@Component({

  selector: 'app-switch',

  templateUrl: './switch.component.html',

  styles: [],

})
export class SwitchComponent implements OnInit {

  constructor() {}

  color = 'RED';

  ngOnInit(): void {}

}
```

*ngSwitchCase is a structural directive because it adds or removes a html element based on a condition.

*ngSwitchDefault is also a structural directive because in this case a default value is added to html DOM in case no switch condition is satisfied.

Q61. Explan Attribute Directive ?

These directives changes behavior or properties of an element.
Attribute directive do not change the DOM structure, It only adds or removes properties of a Html element.
Some commonly used Attribute directives are -
- **ngStyle**
- **ngClass**

Q62. What are ngStyle and ngClass Directives ?

Some commonly used Attribute directives are -

- **ngStyle**
- **ngClass**

<ins>ngStyle</ins> -

ngStyle is a attribute directive which dynamically updates the style of html elements.

e.g.

[.html file]

```html
<div>
  <label for="">Enter Color: </label>
  <input type="text" [(ngModel)]="color">
  <div [ngStyle]="{backgroundColor: color}">Color is {{color}}</div>
</div>
```

<ins>ngClass</ins> -

ngClass is a attribute directive which dynamically adds or removes CSS classes based on a condition.

e.g.

[.css file]

```css
.myColor{
  background-color: red;
}
```

[.html file]

```html
<div>
  <label for="">Enter Color: </label>
  <input type="text" [(ngModel)]="color">
  <div [ngClass]="{myColor: color==='red'}">Color is {{color}}</div>
</div>
```

Q63. What can you tell about Pipes ?

- Pipes transform your output

e.g.

`{{ value | `**`uppercase`**` }}`

Note* : (| Pipe) will transform output to uppercase letters

- Parameters can be passed in pipes using colon(:)

e.g.

`{{ value | `**`date : 'fullDate'`**` | uppercase }}`

- Multiple parameters can be passed using multiple colons (:)
- Custom pipes can be created using **@pipe** decorator
- Computed values in Pipes do not get updated by default. You can add **'Pure'** property to get updated values

Q64. How to create a Custom Pipe ?

- Pipe and PipeTransform libraries need to be imported
- Add **@pipe** decorator
- Override the **transform** method which is implemented from **PipeTransform**

e.g.

```
import { Pipe, PipeTransform } from '@angular/core';

@Pipe({
 name: 'filter',
  pure: false
})
export class FilterPipe implements PipeTransform {

 transform(value: any, filterString: string, propName: string): any {
   // …. custom pipe
 }
}
```

Q65. How to use Services using Dependency Injection ?

- Services can be any reusable typescript class
- We need not create instance of service to use it, instead we be using dependency injector provided by Angular.

<u>Dependency Injector</u>

- Injects dependency (instance of service class) into component
- **Constructors** are used to inject services into components
- Add **providers** property in your component where you want to use service
- **providers** property can be added in **AppModule** to provide application level scope for a service.

e.g.

[App.module.ts]

```
import { BrowserModule } from '@angular/platform-browser';

import { NgModule } from '@angular/core';

import { AppComponent } from './app.component';

import { UserService } from './user/service';

@NgModule({

declarations: [

AppComponent

],

 imports: [

  BrowserModule

],

 providers: [UserService],
```

```
  bootstrap: [AppComponent]

})

export class AppModule { }
```

Q66. What is Hierarchial Injector ?

- Scope of service flows from top to bottom i.e. from highest level (AppModule) to component level
- Service instance in child component will override same instance from parent component.

Q67. What are Nested Services ?

Nested Services

- One service can be injected into other services
- **@Injectable** decorator needs to be added to a receiving service class, where you need to inject another service to it.

Note:-

In new Angular versions, new approach is introduced to provide service in your application .

Instead of using providers array in Appmodule, you can now use

@Injectable({providedIn: 'root'}) in service components to provide application-wide scope.

e.g.
```
import { HttpClient } from '@angular/common/http';
import { Injectable } from '@angular/core';
import { Observable } from 'rxjs';
```

```typescript
@Injectable({
  providedIn: 'root',
})
export class LoginService {
  constructor(private http: HttpClient) {}

  ServiceMethod1() { .... }
  ServiceMethod2() { .... }
}
```

Q68. What are Forms in Angular ?

Forms in Angular are used to handle user's input. It is used for data entry forms like login, register pages etc.

Two approaches for building forms in Angular :

1. Template-driven
2. Reactive

Q69. What is Difference between Template and Reactive ?

Template-driven	Reactive
Form objects are created in Html **DOM**	Form objects are created programmatically in **typescript** file and synchronized with Html DOM elements
Easy Scenarios	Complex Scenarios
Two way data **binding** using **ngModel**	**Immutable** i.e. no data binding since typescript file already have access to form objects
Complex form **validations** are **cumbersome**	Complex form **validations** are **easy** to implement
Imported using **FormsModule**	Imported using **ReactiveFormsModule**

Not easy to test	Easy to test

Q70. Tell me about Template Driven Form ?

<u>Template-driven form</u>

In template-driven forms we write logic, validations, controls etc. in the template part of the code (html file). It uses 2-way binding using ngModel.

e.g.

[.html file]

```html
<form (ngSubmit)="onSubmit(formData)"  #formData ="ngForm">

<div class="form-group">

<label for="username">Username</label>

<input

type="text"

id="username"

class="form-control"

ngModel

name="username"

required

/>

</div>

<button class="btn btn-primary" type="submit">Submit</button>

</form>
```

[.ts file]

```typescript
import { Component} from '@angular/core';

import { NgForm } from '@angular/forms';

@Component({

  selector: 'app-root',

  templateUrl: './app.component.html',

  styleUrls: ['./app.component.css']

})

export class AppComponent {

 onSubmit(formData: NgForm) {

   console.log('submitted form values : ' + formData);

 }

}
```

Q71. How to submit form using ViewChild ?

- **@ViewChild** can be used to avoid passing of local form variable from html form to submit event in typescript file
- **ViewChild** needs to be imported from @angular/core

[.html file]

```html
<form (ngSubmit)="onSubmit()"  #formData ="ngForm">

<div class="form-group">

<label for="username">Username</label>

<input

type="text"

id="username"
```

```html
class="form-control"
ngModel
name="username"
required
/>
</div>
<button class="btn btn-primary" type="submit">Submit</button>
</form>
```

[.ts file]

```typescript
import { Component , ViewChild } from '@angular/core';
import { NgForm } from '@angular/forms';
@Component({
selector: 'app-root',
templateUrl: './app.component.html',
styleUrls: ['./app.component.css']
})
export class AppComponent {
@ViewChild(' formData ') formObject: NgForm;
onSubmit() {
console.log('submitted form values : ' + this.formObject);
}
}
```

Q72. What is Reactive Form ?

Reactive forms provide **model driven** approach to handle user inputs.

Libraries which needs to be imported for reactive forms

1. ReactiveFormsModule
2. FormGroup
3. FormControl
4. Validators (optional :- for validation purpose)

Q73. What are the steps to create a Reactive Form ?

Steps to create reactive forms are : -

1. Declaring form objects in typescript file (.ts file)

e.g.

```
import { FormControl,FormGroup } from '@angular/forms';

export class AppComponent implements OnOnit{

loginForm: FormGroup

ngOnInit()

{

this.loginForm = new FormGroup(

{


  'username': new FormControl(null),

  'email'   : new FormControl(null),

   'gender' : new FormControl('male')

 }

 );
```

}

}

FormControl are key value pairs in which arguments can be passed

1st argument - default value
2nd argument - validators
3rd argument - asyncvalidators

2. Synching Typescript and Html Form Objects (.html file)

e.g.

```html
<form [formGroup]="loginForm" (ngSubmit)="Submit()">

  <input

    id="username"

    formControlName="username"

  />

</form>
```

3. Adding Validations
    - Pass Validators as 2nd argument in FormControl
    - **Validators** needs to be imported '@angular/forms'

e.g.

```typescript
import { FormControl,FormGroup , Validators } from '@angular/forms';

{

this.loginForm = new FormGroup

({

'username': new FormControl(null , Validators.required ),

//Passing multiple validators - Passed as array

'email': new FormControl(null ,[ Validators.required, Validators.email ])
```

) };

}

4. Getting access to controls in Html template

- **get()** :- Get access to controls, by specifying control name or its path.
- e.g.:- loginForm.get('username')

<span

 *ngIf="!loginForm.get('username').valid &&
loginForm.get('username').touched"

 > Validation message

 </span>

Q74. How to Reset a Form ?
Reset the form

this.loginForm.**reset**();

Q75. Tell about Validity States ?
Some of the frequently used states are : -

1. **ng-invalid** - if the field doesn't satisfy validation requirements
2. **ng-valid** - if the field satisfies validation requirements
3. **ng-dirty** - if field values are changed
4. **ng-pristine** - if field values are not changed
5. **ng-touched** - if the field is focused
6. **ng-untouched** - if the field is not focused

e.g.

<span

 *ngIf="!loginForm.get('username').valid && loginForm.get('username').touched"

> Validation message

</span>

Q76. What is Routing ?

- Routes are objects comprised of at least one path and a component
- Routes are objects in which parameters are passed as a key value pairs
- Routes is a array of unique path and component

1. **Path** - refers to the URL of the component
2. **Component** - refers to the component corresponding to a URL specified in path

e.g.

```
const routes: Routes = [

  { path: 'login',  component:  LoginComponent },

];
```

Q77. What are the steps to add a Routing ?

Steps to add routing are : -

1. Register routes

Libraries that needs to be imported for Routing to work :-

1. Routes from '@angular/router'
2. RouterModule from '@angular/router'

```
import { Routes, RouterModule } from '@angular/router';
```

These libraries are usually imported at highest level to provide application level scope.

- Mostly we register routes in AppModule

- Separate Routing Module can also be used to register routing paths

2. Add Placeholder in component

- After registering routes, we need to a add placeholder in a parent component to load different components
- **<router-outlet></router-outlet> is a placeholder**
- Content of Activated component will be loaded inside the **router-outlet** placeholder

3. RouterLink

- Links of routes can be added using RouterLink
- URL specified in routerLink will do pattern matching of this path in router module and will load corresponding component accordingly

e.g.

`<a routerLink = "login">Login</a>`

Now, in the <a> element we can also use href to load route links. But we use routerLink instead of href because of following reasons :-

- RouterLink is faster than href
- RouterLink avoids reloading of page while in href page gets reloaded and all the storages of the page will get lost

routerLink can also be used in **property binding**

e.g.

`<a [routerLink]="['/login']">Login</a>`

using property binding with routerLink, we can pass URL path and multiple parameters corresponding to it easily

4.RouterLinkActive

Now, using routerLink we can traverse to different routes but we will not be able to know which route is currently active .

e.g.

```html
<div>
  <ul class="nav nav-tabs">
    <li>
      <a class="nav-link"
      routerLink="link1"
        routerLinkActive="active">
      Link1</a>
    </li>
    <li>
      <a class="nav-link"
      routerLink="link2"
        routerLinkActive="active">
      Link2</a>
    </li>
    <li>
      <a class="nav-link"
      routerLink="link3"
        routerLinkActive="active">
      Link3</a>
    </li>
  </ul>
</div>
<div></div>
<router-outlet></router-outlet>
```

Note* : Selected link will be set as active dynamically using routerLinkActive

routerLinkActiveOptions :

if we are giving some default path in our routing like "/" then we need to tell angular that link should get active for this particular path only

```
<li [routerLinkActiveOptions]="{exact:true}">

<a routerLinkActive="active" routerLink="/">

Login</a></li>
```

Note* : [routerLinkActiveOptions] will now match the exact path in case of empty path like "" or "/".

5. Navigate

We can also navigate programmatically from typescript file. Let's say we need to load certain routes based on some conditions then in that case we can use **navigate** .

e.g.

```
OnSubmit(): void
{
    this.router.navigate(['link2']);
}
```

Steps to use Navigate : -

1. import router from '@angular/router'
   - import { Router } from '@angular/router';
2. Inject Router in a constructor
   - constructor(private router: Router) { }
3. Use router instance to call navigate method
   - this.router.navigate(['link2']);

Q78. What is a Activated Route ?

<u>Activated route</u>

It signifies the currently active route.

e.g.

```typescript
import { Component, OnInit } from '@angular/core';

import { ActivatedRoute, Router } from '@angular/router';

@Component({

 selector: 'app-link1',

 templateUrl: './link1.component.html',

 styles: [],

})
export class Link1Component implements OnInit {

 constructor(private router: Router, private activeRoute: ActivatedRoute) {}

 ngOnInit(): void {}

 OnSubmit(): void {

  this.router.navigate(['link2']);

 }

 OnReload(): void {

  this.router.navigate(['/link1'], { relativeTo: this.activeRoute });

 }

}
```

Steps to use ActivatedRoute :-

1.   import ActivatedRoute from @angular/router'

import { ActivatedRoute, Router } from '@angular/router';

2.   Inject ActivatedRoute   in a constructor

constructor(private router: Router, private activeRoute: ActivatedRoute) {}

3.   Use the instance in navigate method

 this.router.navigate(['/link1'], { relativeTo: this.activeRoute });

Q79. What are Routing parameter types ?

Routing parameters types

1. Required parameters
2. Optional parameters
3. Query parameters
4. State parameters

Q80. How to fetch route parameters ?

Route parameters can be fetched using following ways : -

snapshot :- Get access to currently active routes' parameters

Snapshot is one of a way to fetch parameters from currently active route

ActivatedRoute :- Get access to currently active route

e.g.

constructor(private activatedRoute: ActivatedRoute) { }

 name = this.activatedRoute.**snapshot**.params['param1'];

Note*: In new Angular versions : -

name = this.activatedRoute.**snapshot**.params.param1;

Q81. How to fetch route parameters reactively ?

- snapshot is appropriate to fetch first initialization of route parameters
- For successive changes **Params observable** should be used

Syntax :

this.activatedRoute.params

.subscribe(

(params: Params) => {

//Fetch route parameters here…

}

);

using **snapshot** we will be getting first initialized data only. Once we reload this page we will still be getting this value and our default value is not updated

To fetch updated values we need to use **Params** observable

Q82. What is paramMap ?

<u>Optional parameters - paramMap</u>

Not mandatory to pass parameter in a routing path while defining them in routing module.

We can use paramMap instead of param to fetch parameters as :-

- It provide more options to fetch parameters like get(), getAll(), has()

- Multiple values corresponding to a parameter can be fetched using paramMap

- paramMap is used in newer versions while param may get depreciated in newer angular versions

paramMap has 3 methods :-

1. **get()** :- it will get the value of specified parameter

    this.getoptionalParam = this.activatedRoute.snapshot.paramMap.get('arg1');

2. **getAll()** :- it will get all values of specified parameter

this.getAlloptionalParam =
this.activatedRoute.snapshot.paramMap.getAll('multiValue');

3. **has()** :- it checks if specified parameter is present in a route

this.hasoptionalParam = this.activatedRoute.snapshot.paramMap.has('arg1');

Q83. What is queryParamMap ?

Optional parameters across any route can be passed using query parameters.

e.g.

OnSubmitQueryParam(): void {

this.router.navigate(['/link5'], { **queryParams**: { arg1: 'value1', arg2: 'value2' ,
multiValue: ['val1', 'val2', 'val3']} });

}

To fetch a parameter : -

this.getqueryParam = this.activatedRoute.snapshot.**queryParamMap**.get('arg1');

Q84. What is State Parameters ?

In new Angular versions we can also pass parameters in a route by using 2nd
argument of navigation method in which we can pass navigation extras.

- **Passing state parameters**

this.router.navigate(['/link1/child1'], {**state: {arg1: id}}**);

- **Fetching state parameters**

```
constructor(private router: Router) {
this.id = this.router.getCurrentNavigation().extras.state['arg1'];
}
```

We will be using getCurrentNavigation() method to fetch state parameters from a route.

points to remember

- Import Router from '@angular/router'

```
import { Router } from '@angular/router';
```

- Constructor should be used to fetch state parameters

Note* : In newer versions argument is passed a property rather than a literal.

```
constructor(private router: Router) {

  this.id = this.router.getCurrentNavigation().extras.state.arg2;

}
```

Q85. What are Routing Fragments ?

- The fragments are optional part of a URL prefixed with a hash (#) symbol
- It is generally used to identify some portion of the URL

Q86. How to pass Fragments ?

Pass fragments

- Passing fragment in html

```
<a [routerLink]="['/link7']" fragment="fragmentData">Link7 - fragments</a>
```

- Passing fragment programmatically

```
this.router.navigate(['/link7'], { fragment: 'fragmentData' });
```

Q87. How to fetch Fragments ?

<u>Fetch fragments</u>

Fetch fragment using **snapshot**

- It will fetch the fragment at the time of initialization of URL

```
this.fragmentParam = this.activatedRoute.snapshot.fragment;
```

Fetch fragment using **subscribe**

- It will fetch the fragment reactively i.e. every time there is a change in fragment, it will fetch updated fragment

```
this.activatedRoute.fragment.subscribe((fragment: string) => {

  this.fragmentSubscribe = fragment;

});
```

Q88. What is Children Route ?

We can also load child components inside parent components by using children property in route configuration.

e.g.

```
path: 'link1',
component: Link1Component,
children: [
{ path: 'child1', component: Child1Component},
{ path: 'child2', component: Child2Component},
]
```

children :- It's a Array of child route objects that specifies a nested route configuration

A placeholder needs to be added in parent component where you want to load a child component

```
<router-outlet></router-outlet>
```

This child route is called in a following way : -

```
this.router.navigate(['/link1/child1'],{state:{arg1: id}});
```

Q89. What is Wild Card Route ?

Wild card route is used to handle any route which is not defined in routes config, we can use wild card (**) routing to handle undefined routes.

e.g.

`{ path: 'anyLink', component: ErrorPageComponent },`

`{ path: '**', redirectTo: 'anyLink' }`

Note* :

- Routes are parsed from top to bottom
- Generic routes like '**' should be placed in last

Q90. What is Router Guards ?

- Router Guards allows or disallows access to route navigations
- Router Guards are executed before a route is loaded or before leaving any route

Q91. What are types of Route Guards ?

There are 4 types of routing guards :-

Route Types	Description
1. canActivate	Validate If a route can be activated
2. canActivateChild	Validate If a child route can be activated
3. canDeactivate	Validate If a user can leave a route
4. Resolve	Load certain data before route is loaded

Q92. Tell about canActivate Guard ?

Validate If a route can be activated

Steps to add route guard in your application :-

1. Add route guard file in your application.
CLI command to add a guard in application
ng g guard route

e.g.
[route.guard.ts]
```
import { Injectable } from '@angular/core';
import {
CanActivate,
ActivatedRouteSnapshot,
RouterStateSnapshot,
UrlTree,
} from '@angular/router';
import { Observable } from 'rxjs';

@Injectable({
providedIn: 'root',
})
export class RouteGuard implements CanActivate {
canActivate(
next: ActivatedRouteSnapshot,
state: RouterStateSnapshot
):
| Observable<boolean | UrlTree>
| Promise<boolean | UrlTree>
| boolean
| UrlTree {
return true;
}
}
```

Step 2 : Now, we need to define which routes needs to be protected by this route
guard

[app-routing.module.ts]

```
{
  path: 'link1',
  canActivate: [RouteGuard],
  component: Link1Component,
  children: [
    { path: 'child1', component: Child1Component},
    { path: 'child2', component: Child2Component}
  ],
},
```

canActivate property is added in route config to provide route guard for a particular route.

Now, RouteGuard will always be activated before 'link1' route is loaded and you can apply any authorization or business logic in RouteGuard that you want to activate before route is loaded.

Q93. What is canActivateChild Guard ?

canActivateChild protects all child routes.

```
e.g.
import { Injectable } from '@angular/core';
import {
CanActivate,
ActivatedRouteSnapshot,
RouterStateSnapshot,
UrlTree, CanActivateChild
} from '@angular/router';
import { Observable } from 'rxjs';

@Injectable({
providedIn: 'root',
```

```typescript
})
export class RouteChildGuard implements CanActivate , CanActivateChild{
canActivateChild(childRoute: ActivatedRouteSnapshot, state:
RouterStateSnapshot):
boolean | UrlTree | Observable<boolean | UrlTree> | Promise<boolean |
UrlTree> {
return false;
}

canActivate(
next: ActivatedRouteSnapshot,
state: RouterStateSnapshot
):
| Observable<boolean | UrlTree>
| Promise<boolean | UrlTree>
| boolean
| UrlTree {
return true;
}
}
```

Now, we need to add canActivateChild hook in route config as well.

[routeConfig]

```typescript
{

path: 'guard',

component: RouteGuardComponent,

canActivateChild: [RouteChildGuard],

children: [

{ path: ':id', component: RouteGuardComponent },

{ path: ':id/:name', component: RouteGuardComponent },

],
```

}

Q94. What is canDeactivate Guard ?

canDeactivate guard is activated before leaving any route. Suppose we want to add some business logic before user navigates away from current route then in that case we can use **canDeactivate** guard**.**

Steps :-

1. Add a canDeactivate guard file in your application.

e.g.

```
import { Injectable } from '@angular/core';

import {

CanDeactivate,

ActivatedRouteSnapshot,

RouterStateSnapshot,

UrlTree,

Router, ActivatedRoute

} from '@angular/router';

import { Observable } from 'rxjs';

@Injectable({

providedIn: 'root',

})

export class CanDeactivateGuard implements CanDeactivate<unknown> {

constructor(private router: Router, private route: ActivatedRoute) {}

canDeactivate(

component: unknown,
```

```typescript
currentRoute: ActivatedRouteSnapshot,

currentState: RouterStateSnapshot,

nextState?: RouterStateSnapshot

):

| Observable<boolean | UrlTree>

| Promise<boolean | UrlTree>

| boolean

| UrlTree {

const result = confirm('Are you sure want to leave this page?');

if (result === false) {

this.router.navigate([currentState.url]);

}

return true;

}

}
```

2. Add canDeactivate hook in routing config

```typescript
{

path: 'guard',

component: RouteGuardComponent,

canActivateChild: [RouteChildGuard],

canDeactivate: [CanDeactivateGuard],

children: [

{ path: ':id', component: RouteGuardComponent },

{ path: ':id/:name', component: RouteGuardComponent },
```

],

}

Q95. What is Resolve Guard ?

- Resolve data before route navigation
- Pre-load certain data before route navigation
- In resolve guard we can actually do some data manipulation and return some kind of data.
- Unlike other guards, resolve guard returns a object

Q96. What are Observables ?

- An Observable is a data source which emits multiple values asynchronously coming from sources like Http requests, events, user input etc.
- Values from Observable are pushed to observers
- Typically asynchronous operations are handled by using Observable
- Lazy loading i.e. It will not be called until it is subscribed
- **RxJs** library is used to import Observable
- Can be unsubscribed to prevent memory leaks by using Unsubscribe method
- Observable (publishers/service) push values to observers (subscribers, client)

Q97. What are parameters needed in subscribe of Obervable ?

The subscribe method **Observable accepts 3 optional functions** as parameters :-

1. **Handle Data** :- Data coming from events raised in sources like Http requests, events, user input etc.
2. **Handle Error** :- Handles any error
3. **Handle Completion** :- Execute any code when Observable is completed

e.g.

```
this.service.getResult()

.subscribe(

   data => this.onSuccess(data),

   error => this.onError(error),

   () => this.onComplete()

);
```

Q98. What are RxJs Operators ?

- RxJs Operators are just function that performs some data manipulations
- RxJs Operators performs action on observable input and returns an observable
- These are pipeable operators i.e. they can be concatenated with subscribe method to get a manipulated output
- RxJs Operators can be imported from 'rxjs/operators' library
- Some of commonly used RxJs Operators are **map, filter, tap** etc.

Q99. Tell about Map Operator ?

- map takes observable as input, perform manipulation on it and returns a new manipulated observable as output
- map **transforms** the emitted values from observable
- map is a **pipeable operator**
- import map from 'rxjs/operators'

e.g.

```
this.route.params.pipe(

map((data: Params) => 'Data ' + data.id
```

```
))

.subscribe(

(data) => {

console.log(data);

},

(error) => {

console.log('Error :' + error);

},

() => {

console.log('Completed...');

}

);
```

Q100. What is Filter Operator ?

- Filter operator will apply some filtration before subscribing the data
- import filter from 'rxjs/operators'

e.g.

```
this.route.params.pipe(

filter((data: Params) => data.id > 4 ),

map((data: Params) => 'Data ' + data.id

))

.subscribe(

(data) => {
```

```
console.log(data);

},

(error) => {

console.log('Error :' + error);

},

() => {

console.log('Completed...');

}

);
```

Q101. What is Operator Chaining ?

Multiple operators can be chained together to send the desired output to subscribe method.

Q102. What is Tap Operator ?

- tap takes observable as input, perform manipulation on it and returns same observable as output
- Purpose of tap is to perform some action without manipulating an observable data
- import tap from 'rxjs/operators'

e.g.

```
this.route.params.pipe(

filter((data: Params) => data.id > 4 ),

map((data: Params) => 'Data ' + data.id),

tap((data) => console.log('Result is :' + data))

)
```

```
.subscribe(

(data) => {

console.log(data);

},

(error) => {

console.log('Error :' + error);

},

() => {

console.log('Completed...');

}

);
```

Q103. What are Http Requests ?

In every application , a backend database source is always required. But we do
not interact with databases directly to prevent security issues. Instead we use API
services for interaction with Database services .Our Angular application will then
interact with API services with the help of Http Requests.

Q104. What are steps to create a Http Request in Angular ?

Steps required to use Http requests in angular application :-

1. Import HttpClientModule in App module class
   ```
   import {HttpClientModule} from '@angular/common/http';
   ```
2. Add this module in imports array to make it available in whole application
   ```
   imports: [
     BrowserModule,
     AppRoutingModule,
     HttpClientModule,
   ```

```
    ],
```
Now, after making HttpClientModule available for whole application , we need to inject the Http Service in a component where we want to use Http Requests

3. We first need to import **HttpClient** from '@angular/common/http'
   ```
   import { HttpClient } from '@angular/common/http';
   ```
4. Then, we can inject **HttpClient** in our constructor to use all the functionalities of a **HttpClient** in a component.
   ```
   constructor(private http: HttpClient) {}
   ```

Q105. What are Http Request verbs in Angular ?

Http request **verbs** :-

1. Post
2. Get
3. Put
4. Delete

1. Post

We use Post requests to add new data in our database

1. In Http post requests, we have 2 required parameters

```
this.http.post('URL Address', body);
```

2. Post requests returns an observable which needs to be subscribed in order to use the data response from API service
3. Without subscribing a Http post request, Angular will not even send this post request.

e.g.: - In the below example, we have a register method in which we are sending a Http post request to our API service

(e.g.:- Any Service class like myService.ts)

```
register()
{
  const body =
  {
    UserName: this.fomModel.value.UserName,
    Email: this.fomModel.value.Email,
  };
  return this.http.post('http://localhost:8080/api/Register', body);
}
```

Now, In Angular without subscribing , it will not even send a post request. So, now we will call this register() method and subscribe it.

```
this.service.register().subscribe(
  (res: any) => {
    console.log('Response data is : ' + res);
  }
);
```

So, like in above example we are subscribing a post request. Now, a post request will be send to a API server.

2. Get

Using Get request, we fetch the data from our database via Api service

- Only 1 parameter is required in Get request

e.g.

```
this.http.get('http://localhost:8080/api/GetData')
```

- Like Post Requests, we also need to **subscribe** Get requests in order to get any response from web API service

```
this.http.get('http://localhost:8080/api/GetData').subscribe(res => {

 console.log(res);

});
```

Note* : Only after subscribing, we will be able to get response from API , otherwise we will not be getting any response.

3. Delete

Delete request is used to delete any data from database.

- Only 1 parameter is required in Get request

```
this.http.delete('http://localhost:8080/api/ClearData')
```

- Again, we need to **subscribe** it to get response from API service

```
this.http.delete('http://localhost:8080/api/ClearData')

.subscribe(res=> {console.log(res);

});
```


4. Put

We use Put requests to update any data in our database via Api

- 2 Parameters are required in Put requests

e.g.

```
update()

{

  const body =

  {

    UserName: this.fomModel.value.UserName,

    Email: this.fomModel.value.Email,
```

```
  };
```

```
  return this.http.put('http://localhost:8080/api/Update', body);
}
```

- We need to **subscribe** it in order to get response from Api service

```
this.service.update ().subscribe((res: any) => {

   console.log('Response data is : ' + res);

  }

 );
```

Q106. How to set custom headers in Http Requests ?

An argument can be passed in all Http Requests (Post, Get, Put, Delete) in which custom header can be defined

- We need to import **HttpHeaders** from '@angular/common/http'

e.g.

```
 .get(

  'http://localhost:8080/api/Update/GetData',

  {

    headers: new HttpHeaders({ 'Custom-Header': 'value' })

  }

 )
```

Note*: {**'Custom-Header': 'value'** } Key-value pair - A custom header name is passed as a key while the value of this header is set as key

Q107. How to pass Query parameter in Http Requests ?

Query parameter can also be passed in Http requests

- We need to import **HttpParams** from '@angular/common/http'

e.g.

```
let myParams = new HttpParams();

myParams = myParams.append('param1');

return this.http

  .get(

   'http://localhost:8080/api/Update/GetData',

   {

     headers: new HttpHeaders({ 'Custom-Header': 'value' }),

     params: myParams

   }

  )
```

Q108. What are Interceptors ?

- Interceptor is a mechanism to **intercept incoming requests** or outgoing response
- By intercepting we can **modify the request or response**
- It act as a middleware between Angular application and Api service
- Interceptor will always get activated before a http request is made. So. some common behavior can be added in interceptor which may be required in all Http requests e.g.:- authentication tokens
- Multiple Interceptors can be added in a application and they execute in same order as provided in module.
- Normally used for logging, authentication, caching , etc. purposes

Q109. How to add a Interceptor in a Angular Application ?

You can either add interceptor class manually or can use CLI command to add interceptor in your application.

CLI command:-

```
ng g interceptor auth
```

CLI command (without test/.spec file)

```
ng g interceptor --skipTests=true auth
```

This will create a following file in your application :-

auth.interceptor.ts

e.g.

[auth.interceptor.ts]

```
import { Injectable } from '@angular/core';
import {
  HttpRequest,
  HttpHandler,
  HttpEvent,
  HttpInterceptor,
} from '@angular/common/http';
import { Observable } from 'rxjs';


@Injectable()
export class AuthInterceptor implements HttpInterceptor {
  constructor() {}
  intercept(
    request: HttpRequest<unknown>,
```

```typescript
  next: HttpHandler
): Observable<HttpEvent<unknown>> {
  // logic here...
  return next.handle(request);
  }
}
```

That is the skeleton of interceptor file. Here you can add your interceptor logic.

Now, we need to tell Angular that we are using a Interceptor service in our application.

3 parameters need to be passed in providers array of AppModule for a interceptor to work.

```typescript
providers: [
  { provide: HTTP_INTERCEPTORS,
    useClass: AuthInterceptor,
      multi: true },
    ]
```

[AppModule.ts]

```typescript
import { AuthInterceptor } from './auth.interceptor';
import { BrowserModule } from '@angular/platform-browser';
import { NgModule } from '@angular/core';
import { AppRoutingModule } from './app-routing.module';
import { AppComponent } from './app.component';
import { HttpClientModule, HTTP_INTERCEPTORS }
from '@angular/common/http';
```

```
@NgModule({

  declarations: [AppComponent, Child1Component],

  imports: [BrowserModule, AppRoutingModule, HttpClientModule],

  providers: [

    { provide: HTTP_INTERCEPTORS, useClass: AuthInterceptor, multi: true },

  ],

  bootstrap: [AppComponent],

})
export class AppModule {}
```

Libraries that needs to be imported are :-

1.   import { HttpClientModule} from '@angular/common/http';

2.   import { HTTP_INTERCEPTORS } from '@angular/common/http';

Q110. How to modify request object in a Interceptor ?

- **Immutable request** - We cannot directly modify a original request in Interceptor
- **Clone** - Need to Clone the request in order to modify it
- **Return modified request** - After modifying a request, we need to return a modified request instead of original request.

e.g.

```
import { Injectable } from '@angular/core';

import {

  HttpRequest,

  HttpHandler,

  HttpEvent,
```

```typescript
  HttpInterceptor,
} from '@angular/common/http';

import { Observable } from 'rxjs';

@Injectable()

export class AuthInterceptor implements HttpInterceptor {

  constructor() {}

  intercept(

    request: HttpRequest<unknown>,

    next: HttpHandler

  ): Observable<HttpEvent<unknown>> {

    const clonedRequest = request.clone({

    headers: request.headers.set('Authorization', 'Bearer ' + '1234')

    });

    return next.handle(clonedRequest);

  }

}
```

Note* : **clone** - We are cloning a request here because without cloning we cannot modify original request

return next.handle(clonedRequest); : - Return a modified request instead of original request.

Using a interceptor , we can use token based authentication and can pass our tokens from interceptors.

Q111. How to handle response in a Interceptor ?

Interceptors always returns an observable which can be piped with operators like map, tap etc. to modify response

e.g.

```typescript
import { Injectable } from '@angular/core';

import { tap } from 'rxjs/operators';

import {

  HttpRequest,

  HttpHandler,

  HttpEvent,

  HttpInterceptor,

  HttpEventType,

} from '@angular/common/http';

import { Observable } from 'rxjs';

@Injectable()

export class AuthInterceptor implements HttpInterceptor {

  constructor() {}

  intercept(

    request: HttpRequest<unknown>,

    next: HttpHandler

  ): Observable<HttpEvent<unknown>> {

    const clonedRequest = request.clone({

      headers: request.headers.set('Authorization', 'Bearer ' + '1234')

    });

    return next.handle(clonedRequest).pipe(
```

```
    tap(
      (success) => {
        if (success.type === HttpEventType.Response) {
          alert('Interceptor response status : ' + success.status);
          alert('Interceptor response body : ' + success.body);
        }
      },
      (error) => {
        alert('Error: ' + error);
      }
    )
  );
  }
}
```

Note* : **Pipe,Tap** - We can pipe the observable with operators like tap if we don't want any modification in our response or map operator to modify response. We get access to properties of response like body, status etc. only if HttpEventType.Response returns a true.

Q112. How to add multiple Interceptors ?

- Multiple interceptors can also be added in a angular application.
- Like we can have authentication and logging interceptor in our application

e.g. :- In the following example we are adding 1 more interceptor in our application (LogInterceptor). We need to add this interceptor in providers array in AppModule

[app.module.ts]

```typescript
import { LogInterceptor } from './log.interceptor';
import { AuthInterceptor } from './auth.interceptor';
import { BrowserModule } from '@angular/platform-browser';
import { NgModule } from '@angular/core';

import { AppRoutingModule } from './app-routing.module';
import { AppComponent } from './app.component';
import { HttpClientModule, HTTP_INTERCEPTORS } from
 '@angular/common/http';

@NgModule({
  declarations: [AppComponent, Child1Component],
  imports: [BrowserModule, AppRoutingModule, HttpClientModule],
  providers: [
{ provide: HTTP_INTERCEPTORS, useClass: LogInterceptor, multi: true },
{ provide: HTTP_INTERCEPTORS, useClass: AuthInterceptor, multi: true }
  ],
  bootstrap: [AppComponent],
})
export class AppModule {}
```

Note* :- **Ordering** is important here. The interceptors are executed in a order in which they are added in providers array.

About the Author

Vishal garg

Vishal Garg is a technical writer with a passion for writing technical books. He has passion for learning new technologies and share the knowledge with everyone. He is well versed in technologies like Azure, Devops, Angular, .Net core, C# etc. He also shares his knowledge with the community through book writings, blog writings , presentations etc.

He has written books on different technologies as well and got a positive reviews on that. He followed a very unique way to cover all major concepts.

With the help of various surveys and real time experience a question bank of a particular topic are compiled and logged in a book.

He is hoping that all readers will be benefited from this book and looking forward to put in more effort to produce quality books in future.

Note : If you like the book, please take some time to put in positive reviews on website. This feedback will encourage him to produce more quality books in future.

More Books by this Author

- .Net Core Simplified: Interview QA

- Angular Simplified: Learning made easy

- C# Interview Question and Answers: Simplified

- Azure Devops: Interview Questions and Answers

www.ingramcontent.com/pod-product-compliance
Lightning Source LLC
Chambersburg PA
CBHW080845160726
47999CB00009B/3014